TOTALLY Silly Science

ABSURD ANIMALS

by Robin Twiddy

BEARPORT PUBLISHING

Minneapolis, Minnesota

CREDITS

Images are courtesy of Shutterstock.com. With thanks to Getty Images, Thinkstock Photo, and iStockphoto.

Recurring images – pics five (paper), Sonechko57 (splats), sebastian ignacio coll (explosion), MoonRock (texture), Ilija Erceg (eyes), Amy Li (illustrations). Cover – Goxy, HSDesain, Eric Isslee, LiveVector, vectorpouch, Nadya_Art. 2–3 – randi_ang, Magicleaf. 4–5 – Doty911, Wise ant, Mooi Design, Ovocheva, Andrey Korshenkov. 6–7 – MIKHAIL GRACHIKOV, Arkadiusz Fajer, rickyd/Shutterstock. 8–9 – Gerald Robert Fischer, Nick Utchin, lukpedclub. 10–11 – Nadya_Art, peart, irin-k. 12–13 – Alexandra Morrison Photo, StefanieMueller, LuckyVector. 14–15 – CoSveta, Ekaterina Kapranova, Don Mammoser. 16–17 – lukpedclub, Noel Powell, photomaster, Alfmaler. 18–19 – John A. Anderson, Simagart, Your_universe. 20–21 – Swaroop Pixs. 22–23 – ffennema/iStock Lisa F. Young, Martin Pelanek. 24–25 – Golden Vector, Ken Griffiths, kezza. 26–27 – Zaie, Daniel Eskridge, Your_universe. 28–29 – tynyuk, Iryna Kalamurza, Happy monkey, Wise ant. 30 – Jan Stria.

Library of Congress Cataloging-in-Publication Data is available at www.loc.gov or upon request from the publisher.

ISBN: 979-8-88822-016-0 (hardcover)
ISBN: 979-8-88822-204-1 (paperback)
ISBN: 979-8-88822-331-4 (ebook)

© 2024 Booklife Publishing
This edition is published by arrangement with Booklife Publishing.

North American adaptations © 2024 Bearport Publishing Company. All rights reserved. No part of this publication may be reproduced in whole or in part, stored in any retrieval system, or transmitted in any form or by any means, electronic, mechanical, photocopying, recording, or otherwise, without written permission from the publisher.

For more information, write to Bearport Publishing, 5357 Penn Avenue South, Minneapolis, MN 55419.

CONTENTS

Serious Science 4
Koala Crimes 6
Mantis Punch 8
Rat LOL 10
Wandering Wonder Dog 12
Walking on Water 14
Pigeons at the Pictures 16
Pom-Pom Pow! 18
Tears of Blood 20
Slime Clothes 22
Liar, Lyre! 24
The Escaping Octopus 26
Totally Silly 28
Glossary 31
Index 32
Read More 32
Learn More Online 32

SERIOUS SCIENCE

Science is always serious, right? Wrong! Science can be anything but stiff and boring.

Animals can be very silly. And the science around them is no different!

You are about to enter the Silly Zone. Learn all about animals doing the strangest things. Get ready for some silly science!

KOALA CRIMES

A koala bear nearly ruined some police work just by touching things!

No two people have the same **fingerprints**. That means police can find out who did a crime by collecting prints nearby. It turns out, koalas also have fingerprints.

Imagine you are a detective. You find fingerprints. But they don't match any of the **suspects**.

They are a koala's fingerprints! But the koala didn't do it! Now, the real criminal is getting away.

MANTIS PUNCH

Is the world record for the fastest punch held by a human? **NO!**

A creature only 4 inches (10 cm) long is the champ! It is the mantis shrimp. This little guy can punch fast enough to break glass!

The mantis shrimp's punch is so fast that scientists can't even see it.

They have to use high-speed cameras. The film also shows a small flash of light with each punch.

RAT LOL

Some scientists tickle rats and get paid for it. Why?

Rats laugh when you tickle them. Scientists who study them have learned a lot.

Laughing may change the way rats think. Rats who were tickled made better decisions.

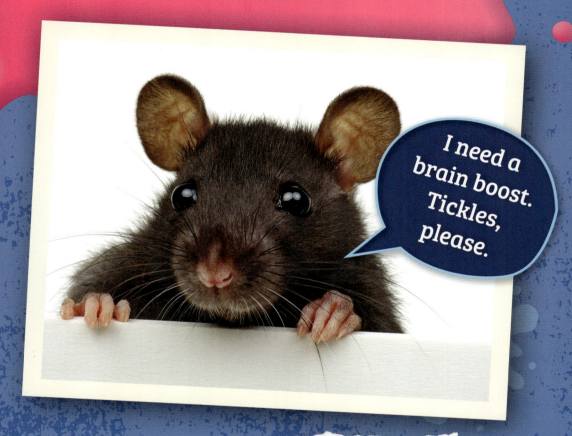

Scientists believe this work helps us understand more about humans.

WANDERING WONDER DOG

A dog named Bobbie got lost during a family vacation. He traveled more than 2,550 miles (4,100 km) to get home.

HOW DID HE DO IT?

Bobbie made it home after six months. He walked the entire journey, making his way across rivers and mountains.

Scientists believe dogs use smell to find their way. Dogs can follow a smell for up to 10 miles (16 km).

Bobbie's family stopped often on their way home. Bobbie followed and stopped at all the same places! Scientists think the smart dog followed the smell from one stop to the next.

WALKING ON WATER

Could you ever walk on water? Only with the right feet! That's how the basilisk lizard does it.

A basilisk lizard has extra scales between the toes on its back legs. It moves quickly, and its special feet stay on top of the water.

The lizards' feet also trap air bubbles. Basilisk lizards can run on water for up to 15 feet (4.6 m) at a time.

Scientists are hoping to use this information to find new ways for people to travel across water.

PIGEONS AT THE PICTURES

Have you ever wondered why you never see pigeons at the movies?

This is so boring!

It is because pigeons can't see videos! To a pigeon, a film looks like a bunch of still images.

Movies show **24** pictures, called frames, every second. Small changes between frames make it look like the pictures are moving.

CINEMA

But pigeons aren't fooled by the **illusion**. These birds would need to see 75 frames per second to think a picture was moving.

POM-POM POW!

This little crab may look like a cheerleader. However, those are not pom-poms. They are live animals called sea anemones!

Anemones have lots of stinging **tentacles**. Pom-pom crabs use them when they punch their enemies.

The anemone's sting can help pom-pom crabs fight off **predators** or even catch lunch.

A sea anemone

Pom-pom crabs are also known as boxer crabs. With the anemones' help, they are fighting champs!

TEARS OF BLOOD

The horned lizard has spiky skin that helps it stay safe. What else does it do for protection?

It has a bloody way to stop predators. It shoots the stuff right from its eyes!

The horned lizard squirts tears of blood directly into the mouths of enemies. But this is no taste test.

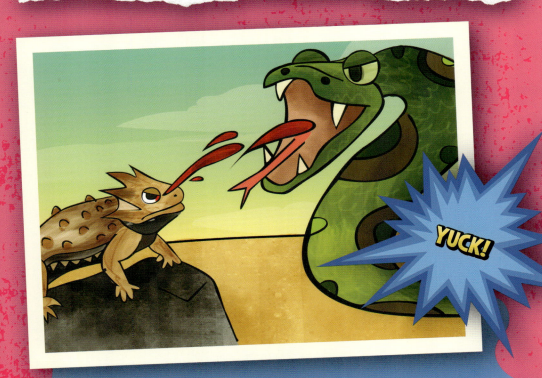

The blood from these lizards has a really *bad* taste. This is because of a **chemical** found inside it.

SLIME CLOTHES

How would you feel if your clothes were made of slime? You might feel sticky . . . or just plain disgusted!

There is a fish in the ocean with a special skill. It makes a slime that is almost as strong as a cotton cloth.

The hagfish uses slime as a defense. When an enemy is near, the fish covers it in gooey slime.

Scientists believe the slime can be useful. They might even try to create it in a lab to make slime clothes!

LIAR, LYRE!

In the Australian forests, you can hear sounds from many different animals. Or maybe it's just a lyrebird!

The lyrebird can **mimic** almost any sound it has heard before. It mostly copies the songs of other birds nearby.

Scientists were surprised by how well the lyrebird copies sounds. But sometimes, the birds can do even more.

One lyrebird at a zoo learned to mimic the sounds of workers' tools, such as drills and hammers. It made these sounds for weeks after the workers left.

THE ESCAPING OCTOPUS

Inky the octopus lived at a New Zealand aquarium. Then, he decided to head back to the ocean.

Octopuses do not have any bones. Because of this, they can squeeze through very small spaces. That's just what Inky did.

Workers think Inky fit through a small gap in his tank. Then, he escaped down a drainpipe.

Scientists know octopuses are smart. Inky must have used his super smarts to make it back to his watery home.

TOTALLY SILLY

Animals can be silly, but so can scientists. You get something strange when you put them both together.

We learned rats laugh when they are tickled. We also learned not to mess with shrimp.

Scientists are thinking about walking on water and making clothes from slime. But is there a point to all the silliness?

Yes! Scientists learn lots of useful things when they do silly science with animals!

It would seem that silly scientists + silly animals = serious science! Well, at least it does sometimes.

WHICH ANIMALS DO YOU THINK ARE THE SILLIEST?

GLOSSARY

chemical a natural or human-made substance that can sometimes be harmful

fingerprints marks made by pressing the tip of a finger on a surface

illusion something that looks or seems different than what it really is

mimic to copy very closely

predators animals that hunt and eat other animals

suspects people who may have done a crime

tentacles long, flexible body parts that are usually used for catching food

INDEX

anemones 18–19
crabs 18–19
dogs 12–13
hagfish 23
horned lizards 20–21
koalas 6–7
lyrebirds 24–25
octopuses 26–27
pigeons 16–17
predators 19–20
rats 10–11, 28
scientists 9–11, 13, 15, 23, 25, 27–29
shrimp 8–9, 28

READ MORE

Finan, Catherine C. *Animals (X-treme Facts: Science).* Minneapolis: Bearport Publishing Company, 2021.

Hyde, Natalie. *Animal Oddballs (Astonishing Animals).* New York: Crabtree Publishing Company, 2020.

LEARN MORE ONLINE

1. Go to **www.factsurfer.com** or scan the QR code below.
2. Enter **"Absurd Animals"** into the search box.
3. Click on the cover of this book to see a list of websites.